INGLIS LECTURES
IN SECONDARY EDUCATION

THE SCHOOL IN AMERICAN
CULTURE

The Inglis Lecture, 1950

The School in American Culture

BY

MARGARET MEAD

CAMBRIDGE
HARVARD UNIVERSITY PRESS
1951

THE
INGLIS LECTURESHIP

To honor the memory of Alexander Inglis, 1879-1924, his friends and colleagues gave to the Graduate School of Education, Harvard University, a fund for the maintenance of a Lectureship in Secondary Education. To the study of problems in this field Professor Inglis devoted his professional career, leaving as a precious heritage to his co-workers the example of his industry, intellectual integrity, human sympathy, and social vision. It is the purpose of the Lectureship to perpetuate the spirit of his labors and contribute to the solution of problems in the field of his interest. The lectures on this foundation are published annually by the School.

THE SCHOOL IN AMERICAN
CULTURE

TO DO JUSTICE to the subject of the school in American culture in the space of a short essay places upon the writer the necessity of focusing sharply on certain aspects of the question. I would like to discuss the teacher within the school, the teacher within the school within a changing society, how her role has been defined and underwritten, what she must learn and unlearn and sometimes learn again in the course of one teaching lifetime.

The anthropologist deals with tradition as it is embodied in the living habituated bodies of the human beings who make up the society which shares that tradition[1]—in their gestures, their words, their expectations, in the images which the words evoke in speaker and in listener. For detailed material the anthropologist would go to particular schools in particular towns and cities, become familiar with particular teachers and their pupils, the parents of the pupils, the citizenry and its school board. The schoolhouse would be mapped and charted, the places of each pupil in school noted so that one would know what happened between the larger and the smaller children, the weak-eyed or the nimble-witted, the laggard and the scholar. But for an over-all picture such as I wish to present tonight, the stuff with which I must work is the cultural experience and expectation of each member of an audience such as this, born and bred in many different parts of the country; taught, disciplined, inspired, or discouraged by many different sorts of teachers, bringing to the words "school" and "teacher" different idiosyncratic versions of the common experience which we can call American, reinterpreting it and sharing it with others, because we hold in common a way of perceiving and understanding experience which is our culture.

Perhaps it will be clearer if we consider for a moment what the ideas "teacher" and "school" have meant in other cultures, let us say in two cultures both of which have been singularly devoted to learning, the culture of the Chinese and of the Eastern European Jews. Among the Chinese[2]—in the village—the teacher was traditionally a poor relation or a stranger, a man who had failed to obtain a high enough rank in his examinations to win a place in the civil service and who was held in low esteem by the village community. To him was delegated the distasteful task of disciplining little boys into learning the hundreds of characters which must be mastered if anyone of them was to escape from the life of the village into the wider scene.

If we turn to Eastern European Jewry,[3] to the small towns or the Jewish quarters of large towns, we find again that learning was reverenced but the teacher who had to make a living from teaching, rather than from being a great scholar who gave freely of his knowledge and wisdom, was accorded no honor. And he in turn made life a misery for the little boys, boys often so small that they had to be carried to school, where they sat in cold, undecorated rooms pouring over tattered, inexplicable schoolbooks written in a language different from that which was their daily speech, a language which their mothers seldom understood at all. The teacher's weapons were an unbelievable vocabulary of sarcasm and vituperation; only one day a year were the devoted small boys permitted to go out into the fields; for all the rest of the year they studied, learning by heart great masses of sacred materials which they did not yet understand. And here, writes the anthropologist who himself was a product of such a school, "the love of learning was born."

Even this very slight reference to other cultures throws into immediate relief how different our schools are—how neither schoolroom nor teacher nor pupils can possibly be described in the same terms, or filled in with the same images. Sights and sounds and smells, the balance of give and take in the relations between teacher and pupils, among the pupils, and between parents and teachers all contrast sharply. And it is through such contrasts that the anthropologist, or any sophisticated student of other societies, is able to distinguish those aspects of any subject which may be said to be not only "cultural," in the sense that they are learned within the stream of human tradition, but "American," in that they are part of what Americans learn, either as children or by those who, born in another culture, come later to this country.

The teacher of whom I shall speak will be necessarily not an average, not a statistical representation of the teachers of the United States at the present time, but rather a distillate of American ideas of the teacher, which is itself compounded from both stereotpye and actual experience, from the teacher in the sentimental song and on the comic valentine, the teacher met on the tourist ship, as well as the teachers of one's own school days, and the teacher from whom one's children or grandchildren are learning. I want to place the image of this American schoolteacher before you with full recognition that schoolteachers in the United States are of many different ages, come from many different backgrounds, are of both sexes, were trained in many different types of normal schools and colleges, and conceive of their teaching in many different ways. But when the American hears the word "schoolteacher"—to the extent that he fills it in in a general way and not merely with an image of Miss Jones of the fourth grade, to whom he took flowers or who caught him smuggling worms into class—the image will be something like this. He will think of a grade-school teacher who teaches perhaps the third or fourth grade; this teacher will be a woman of somewhat indeterminate age, perhaps in the middle thirties, neither young nor old, of the middle class, and committed to the ethics and manners of a middle-class world. In the emotional tone which accompanies the image there will be respect, a little fear, perhaps more than a little affection, an expectation that she will reward his efforts and struggles to learn and conform, and a spate of delighted memories of those occasions when he himself perpetrated feats of undetected mischief. She stands in his mind on the borderline of childhood, urging, beckoning, exhorting, patiently teaching, impatiently rebuking a child in whom the impulse is strong to escape the narrow bounds of the school room into the outdoors where birds are nesting, or the sun-lit pavements are waiting for marbles. The phrase "teacher said" or "teacher wants" can revivify in the aged this sense of borderline pressure, this figure outside the home, the representative of society, urging, helping, poking, scolding, encouraging those whose "steps though lagging slow to school, went storming out to playing."

The teacher herself, as well as those whom she taught or teaches now, is subject to this same image. If she is younger than the image, she is conscious of herself as a "young teacher," if older, her graying hair classifies her as an "old teacher." Because the image is of a spinster, if she is married, then in her mind and others she is a "married teacher" or a "married woman who is still teaching." The man who teaches in grade school has to deal with a self-classification of being a "man teacher," thus tacitly acknowledging that his is a male version of a role which is felt to be feminine. Teachers who are members of any group who are in a minority in their particular community will have to add—in their own minds —that they are Negro teachers or Japanese teachers, Catholic or Jewish or Protestant teachers, as the case may be, redefining themselves against an image of a woman who, for most of the country, is white, middle-class, middle-aged, and of Protestant background. So when I use the word "teacher," it will be with a recognition of this image, informed, of course, with the known facts of age range and class origin which have been collected and analyzed from time to time concerning the actual teaching group in the United States.[4]

When we turn from the teacher to the school, we again have a series of images. From this series three may be selected as useful, the little red schoolhouse, the academy, and the city school with its narrow cement schoolyard in which the children of immigrants mill about in a space too small for play. The little red schoolhouse, which exists today only in backward and forgotten areas of the country, is still the symbol of a stable, democratic, slowly changing, real American world. Here the teacher, herself often a mere slip of a girl, a young teacher, wrestles with her slightly younger contemporaries, boards with members of the school board, is chaperoned by the entire community of whom she is really one, and finally marries a member of that community —or goes on teaching forever with, happily, at least one attributed romance to give her dignity and pathos. For the teacher in the little red schoolhouse is not an old maid whom no man wishes to marry; she is a girl who is a little more intelligent, a little better educated, and more alert than the others, who will herself be very selective in marriage, and who may therefore in the end remain unwed. But she belongs within the community in which she teaches, a community which in the image is stylized, being without class structure, but made up of people who are more or less worthy and substantial, thrifty or shiftless, with large farms and well-kept fences, or small farms overrun by blackberry vines. She teaches the children pretty much what their parents learned; new teaching is viewed with suspicion, and the school board of the little red schoolhouse are traditionally regarded as the enemies of all change. Some schooling is conceded to be necessary, parents do not have time to do it, so one of their number is hired to teach what the parents know, or at least once learned for a little while, to the children. Parents and teacher are thoroughly in league as far as the child is concerned, standards of school and home are the same, and a "licking at home meant a licking at school." The school is a one-room school, the big pupils help the little ones, and the brighter little ones listen while the older pupils recite. In such a school, the gifted twelve-year old immigrant boy learns enough in a year to be an American. In such a school, mischief is innocent and sacred, the pranks against the teacher are as traditional as her reprisals, the struggle between the young teacher and the overgrown boy who is tired of book learning represents the victory of common sense and adulthood over the school room.

This image, the beloved image of the school, crops up in the minds of those who have never in fact seen such a school, so firmly is it rooted in our literature and tradition. Like so many of the symbols of the American dream, it stands both for a desirable state never attained and for a past golden age which has been lost—the school in a world which did not change, a world of rural images, where "blackberry vines are running" and goodness was literally symbolized by a "clean slate."

Beside this image, we must place two other schools. There is the academy, at which the children of the privileged were initiated into the mysteries of our heritage from Europe, Latin, Greek, music; the school to which the parents who could afford it sent their children, so that their children would remain part of the past to which they owed, or wished to owe, allegiance. Where the perspective of the little red school-house was limited to the childhood of the parents themselves, with its folk statement, "What was good enough for me is good enough for my child," the perspective of the academy stretched back to the culture of the grandparents and great grandparents who had been judges and governors. Here the aspiration of the parent who wished to give his child not "what was enough for me," but "the advantages of a fine education" which was customary in his family, mingled with the aspiration of the parent who wished to give his child something better than he himself had had. Both aspirations sought to structure the future in terms of the past, to guarantee the child's future position by the degree to which he participated in the heritage of the past. Teachers in academies were more likely to be men than women, thus again symbolizing the relationship to Europe, rather than the new America where men were so busy building a new world that the "finer things of life" had to be left to women.

The third image is that of the city school, on the built-up street, a school so lacking in architectural personality that it would be almost impossible to represent one without the presence of the mass of children, crowded on the sidewalk, milling in the narrow playground. These children are the children of immigrants. They are not only poor, but they are foreign; they have unpronounceable names and eat strange things for breakfast; their mothers come with shawls over their heads to weep and argue and threaten a teacher who is overworked, whose nerves are frayed by the constant battle with the polyglot youngsters who surge through her classroom.

The classroom is crowded; through the windows nothing can be seen except another wall. Around the blackboard there is a pitiful row of cut-out bunnies, or on the blackboard a devoted but over-worked teacher has traced Santa Claus and his reindeer. The children's speech is a babble of broken American; they must be taught to spell words they have never heard, to read about fairy-tale heroines and historical figures whose very names are strange to their parents. They must be taught to wash, to brush their teeth, to drink milk, to value time, to write a letter. They must be taught, not the constancies of their parents' immediate past, as in the little red schoolhouse, or the precious values of a long ancestral past, as in the academy, but they must be taught to reject, and usually to despise, their parents' values. They must learn those things which, to the extent that they make them Americans, will alienate them forever from their parents, making them an-cestorless, children of the future, cut off from the past.

In any discussion of American schools, of "the American school system," of "the public school," if you listen carefully, you can see these images come and go, the loved and longed-for image of the little red schoolhouse, the deprecated and worried-over image of the city school, and the image of the private academy, which contains all of America's ambivalence about England, about tradition, about class. The affectionate note with which the little red schoolhouse is invoked is a statement of our sense of conflict between the academy that perpetuates the past— which in American terms means limiting the future, tying us to the old world and its caste lines and age-old solutions—and the city school which belongs only to the future, which turns out pupils who, because they cannot look back, have, in a sense, no perspective at all, but only the dreadful urgency of moving on, moving away from, knowing only that what was once theirs by birthright is bad and un-American, that what is NOT that, what is new and up to the minute, must therefore be American and good.

All three of these themes have become inter-woven in our contemporary American culture so that a tenth-generation American,[5] educated in private schools, will have difficulty persuading his child, who has learned to speak Spanish from an upper-class but foreign mother, that it is not something shameful and disgraceful to be heard speaking a foreign tongue on the street. And the contrast between the mischief of the country boy and the delinquency of the immigrant slum boy has vanished too, so that the select suburb in which tenth-generation Americans and success-ful third-generation Americans live side by side has its juvenile delinquents also. It has its quarrels among the parent taxpayers as to whether foreign languages are to be taught in the schools, its conflicts as to whether the teacher is to be treated as an equal, as the emissary of a strange outside world, or as the poorly paid custodian of the gateway to "culture."

If we turn from images to look formally at the history of American education, of its theory and its practice, the conflict between the school oriented toward the past and the school oriented toward the future, with the seldom obtainable dream of a school which would hold the world steady, will be found to be a prevailing theme. This theme is expressed in many forms: in the struggle between the classics and modern languages; in the struggle between "at least one foreign language" and none at all; in the struggle between academic studies and vocational preparation; in the arguments about required courses versus electives, in which shared conformity to a common past is opposed to selectivity which is a preparation for an unshared future.

Before I go on to discuss the part which this threefold picture of the school has played and is playing in American educational theory and practice, I should like to turn for a moment to the contrasts and comparisons provided by primitive societies on the relationships between the generations. Primitive societies are our models for slowly changing homogenous societies[6] in which the children's lives faithfully repeat, gesture for gesture, and experience by experience, the lives of their parents and grandparents. Through the investigation of such slowly changing societies, we can form a picture of type relationships between the old generation and the new, against which such relationships, when they occur in an age of rapid change like our own, take on additional meaning. In these slowly changing primitive societies we find great variation as to which age group inducts the young child into his society; the baby may spend most of its time with its mother or father, or in the arms of an older sister or brother, or by the side of a grandmother or grandfather. Each is a possible way to learn the intricate, beautifully patterned way of perceiving the world and acting within that set of perceptions which a culture offers each child born within it.

But if we examine in detail some of the implications of the parent-child, sibling-child, and grandparent-child rearing situations, we find certain systematic differences. Those societies in which young children are reared by grandparents[7] —of which certain North American Plains Indian tribes are typical— have an enormous degree of conservatism. The culture survives, even as the buffalo disappear; the land is taken away by the advancing white peoples, and the tepee is displaced by the shack. Still the language, the way of thought, of the past endures. Sometimes we find only one or two survivors of a whole language group, two toothless, half-deaf old women, who will, however, have clung to their language and their memories, and are still able to dictate long texts to the patient ethnographer. This conservatism, this cherishing clinging to the old, can be related to the role which the grandparent played in the lives of Indian children, to the way in which the child, even as it struggled and wriggled in an ecstasy of beginning movement, apprehended in the tonus of the grandparental arms the sort of pact which its lively little body would someday make with death. As old hands and old voices, speaking with the gentleness and resignation of a people who saw human lives as like grass which grew up in the morning and at night was mown down, informed the child of the way that men and animals, the sun and the moon and the stars, seeking and power, vision and practicality, life and death were to be viewed, so the child was able to incorporate in early childhood all that his culture had to offer him. In such a rounded understanding, nothing was left unexplained, uncontemplated, which later would challenge or threaten. And the Indian has remained as one of our chief examples of the tenacity of a people who, robbed of every condition of their lives, still clung to the form, to the pattern, meeting night after night to gamble for buffalo nickels where once the stake was a war horse.

At the opposite extreme, we find the cultures in which it is the child nurse—the elder sister or less frequently the elder brother—who carries the younger child about on a hip almost too slight to bear the burden.[8] Instead of the tremor of old age, there is the tenseness of the hands which can hardly lift, the hands which are almost unable to readjust the carrying sling, or shift the baby from one hip to another. These child nurses, far from having learned the nature of the whole life cycle from their old grandmothers, are just out of babyhood themselves, and were reared by other children. The child on the hip is not something infinitely young and remote, waiting at the end of memory, but the child whom one was yesterday, with all the fears and urgencies which have just been partially mastered in the self. These are the cultures in which the growing child is kept close to infancy, sometimes only by way of keeping a great awareness of the rhythms of its own body, so that later dancing and love-making will be equally easy and graceful, as in Samoa.[9] Sometimes also the child is kept close to the images of infancy, so that the ritual resolutions of its early terrors are expressed in the theater by conflicts between witch and dragon, who re-ënact on a stage the conflicts which the child experiences in its relationship to father and mother, as in Bali.[10] Or the child nurse may help the child retain its passivity, in a world where every adult is egging it on to continuous unre-mitting displays of energy and anger, as among the Iatmul.[11] Among this head-hunting tribe of the Sepik River, where adult relationships are violent and assertive, the theater is a series of tableaux in which all movement is frozen and static, in contrast to the theater of Bali where a people whose daily life is ordered and gentle are able to express the most violent emotions. In the spontaneous drawings[12] and in the play of the children of the child-nurse age we can find the links which permit their child charges to retain the feeling that makes the adult theatrical pres-entation both possible and meaningful, as the Balinese child keeps alive the capacity for plastic expression of feeling and the Iatmul child, who in his adult life must be stormy and noisy, keeps his capacity for stillness.

The child nurse may be seen not as the guardian and ally of any particular aspect of early childhood, but rather as a way in which the child's response within its culture is kept intact in spite of the pressures which will later fall upon the adolescent and the adult. From the child nurse there passes to the native child a kind of license to be itself, from one who has not yet departed far enough from that closeness to the experience of early childhood to be able to withdraw the license. And so we have a second model, the society in which the resources of early childhood, whether in directness of bodily expression or richness of phantastic elaboration or denial of the adult structuring of the world, are preserved for children, and therefore for adults also, because the child learns not from someone who has traversed the whole round of life, but from someone still very close to its beginning.

The two models of child and grandparent upbringing are brought together again when we consider the aristocratic society in which the upper-class child has a nurse drawn from the peasantry and in which the child of the peasant class is cared for by its grandmother, while the mother works in the fields. Here, the peasant child, like the Plains Indian child, is exposed to the whole of the culture which will be its for life, caught tightly in a mesh that it cannot break, born a peasant to die a peasant. In the same society the same type of peasant woman, not always so old, is performing quite a different function for the child of the aristocrat, keeping alive in it impulses and dreams which its more educated, differently controlled parents would, if they were its mentors, disallow.[13] So the peasant nurse keeps alive in the aristocratic child his sense of his own body and himself, which can then tolerate the rigors of court etiquette, rigid demands for posture and gesture, for honor and conformity to the demands of caste; while, as a peasant she communicates to her own grandchild a way of life in which body and self play a different part, upon a simpler stage.

The third model, the model which echoes the little red schoolhouse image, is that in which children are reared not by grandparents who represent the whole traditional definition of life, or by children whose own eager little mouths have hardly left the breast, or by nurses whose own peasant standards of eating and drinking perpetuate the pleasures of the breast with a frank enjoyment which is banished from ballroom and audience chamber, but by parents, by people of early maturity, the present possessors and inheritors of the adult world. This is the typical middle-class position: a family economically well enough off so that the mother is not burdened down with field or farm duties—or overwhelmed with more children than she can feed and care for, in which the father is making his way, actively, in a world of change and commerce, a world of entrepreneurship and profit. In such a rapidly changing world, grandparents are likely to be out of date, behind the times, and also to a degree rejected, as it was they who reared the present parents, and reared them purposefully and determinedly to become responsible, time-bound, goal-oriented adults. In such a world also elder siblings are busy themselves learning to outstrip their parents. They have too much to do to be efficient baby tenders; they must learn the skills and arts which will be necessary for success. Furthermore, the middle-class parent will distrust the child nurse, as also the servant girl is distrusted. The child who is to be inducted into a world where life is real and life is earnest must be exposed from the beginning to the model parent, who must herself, and himself, punish and reward the growing child. This middle-class picture is not only true of our own American middle-class life, but also can be found in primitive societies like that of the Manus of the Admiralities,[14] a tribe of stone-age fishermen. The Manus are efficient, profit-seeking, earnest, moral people, concerned to rear their children to follow the same pattern—not so much of life, as of goal seeking. And among the Manus the older children practice in play the arts of adult life, and the parents care for the children, who learn to think of adults as persons who are completely masters of their environment.

The child who is reared according to this third model—reared by parents who are at the height of their careers, far from childhood, and facing an old age about which they know little and expect little—grows up, far from its infant awareness of its body, far from the memory of the childhood fantasies which fed eagerly and hungrily on the very meagre set of symbols which such a culture possesses, but alert and ready to face a relatively new and uncharted world, in a thoroughly learned and throughly charted way. Close contact with the grandparent leaves little room for welcoming change or sailing strange seas. Close contact with child nurse or peasant nurse keeps the child so *en rapport* with its body and the arts and rituals whose meanings it is able to retain that it also will be, on the whole, uninterested in change and conquest. But parent-rearing produces a child who faces toward a partial future, who can conceive life as an unwritten chapter of a book that is unfinished.

But these three models which I have been discussing are models drawn from slowly changing homogeneous societies; I have been able to speak of a life in which those who rear were similarly reared, in which all the lullabies one sings to children are the lullabies one heard as a child. If such models are to be of any use in considering the problem of the teacher in the American school today, we must add to them from the actual situation in our own society, the condition of rapid change. We must add to them both the reflection in all adults, whether of the parent or of the grandparent generation, the changes through which they have passed, the fact that they were reared by parents whose hands were already fumbling before unfamiliar doors, or with hands which lay flaccid with despair in a world they had not dreamed of and could not cope with.[15] We must picture the adult who has been reared in a dozen tones of voice, reprimanded, rewarded, cajoled, and teased and appeased according to half a hundred systems, who has learned to move about somehow, in a series of rooms in which the very arrangement of the furniture either diagrams the lack of harmony in the tastes which gradually assembled it or in its perfection of harmony will give him a pattern which he is not likely to repeat. And to this picture of an adult who in personality is the expression of the great heterogeneity and rapid changes in our current society, we must add the picture of children who differ from the children who came ten years before them, and differ also from the children who will follow them, as children reared on schedules are followed by children rocked to sleep, to be in turn succeeded by children reared according to some new one of the prescriptions through which a newly self-conscious society is attempting to meet newly realized needs. The condition in our society to-day is dramatized by the late-born child, whose mother finds that nothing that she learned ten years ago about how to treat children or of what to expect from them, can be applied to this newcomer, who seems even to have learned to cry with a new note in its voice, who will have to have different clothes, will display different tastes, and will weep for quite different reasons. Where, in slowly changing societies, the adults are confronted by children whom they know—for were they not such children themselves, just such children with the same fears, the same joys, the same bits of mischief and rebellion—the adults in the modern world face children who are not only unlike their own past childhood, but who are actually unlike any children who have ever been in the world before.

How then does the teacher—the teacher who may stand at the door of the academy, or its successor the academic high school, ready to induct these unknown children into the tradition of the past, and the teacher who stands at the

door of the crowded slum school, ready to prepare her pupils to enter the future by leaving
their past—how does this teacher fit into the
changing world in which she is called upon to
play so sensitive and significant a role?

We may consider for a moment the way in
which the teacher can approximate to each of the
three generation positions: the grandparent who
has seen the whole of life, the parent who is living
it day by day, and the child or nurse who is the
custodian not of the child's future so much as
of the child's immediate past.

The type teacher who comes closest to the
grandparental role is the teacher of the classics,
or the teacher who treats mathematics and science
as if they were classics, fixed and immutable, as
unchanged and unchanging as the figures on
Keats' Grecian urn. The gifted teacher of the
classics conveys to the child a sense of the round-
edness and relatedness of life, of the way in which
each period repeats in its own way an old story
that has already been written in a more gracious
and finished way in the past. Any budding desire
to explore the new, to make new conquests, can
be gently, benignly reduced to the expected, by
a reference to Diogenes or to Alexander. As man
has been, man will be; one can learn to write
different but not better sonnets in a world which
has dignity and form. The teacher in the academy

was typically such a teacher laying the ground-
work for an orderly acceptance of a world which,
however different today's version seemed, was
mercifully never new.

The teacher in the overcrowded city school—
where there were too few seats and too few books
in a room filled with strange smells from foreign
eating habits and foreign sleeping habits—is
closest to the parent model, as she struggles to get
her pupils to face away from the past and toward
the future. She teaches her pupils to acquire
habits of hygiene and of industry, to apply themselves diligently to prepare to succeed, and to
make the sacrifices necessary to success, to turn
a deaf ear to the immediate impulse, to shatter
any tradition which seems to block the path to
the goal, but to shatter it in a way and with the
sanctions of the entrepreneur. This teacher is
closest to the model in which the parents rear the
child to a kind of behavior rather than to fit within a tradition. When she imitates the teacher of
the academy and teaches her pupils to learn
memory gems, she will find she faces confusion,
because she is teaching them the past of older
Americans in order to give them a future, and
this contains contradictions. How will these
children born in hospitals, treated at clinics, who
celebrate a holiday in the biggest movie theater,
use such memory gems as "I remember, I remem-

ber the house where I was born," or "over the river and through the wood to grandfather's house we go; the horse knows the way to carry the sleigh through the white and drifting snow"? She will be happiest when she teaches modern history, with the next pages still to be written, in a "current events" class; or when she teaches science as a way of looking at life which is constantly changing, constantly discarding what has been the best hypothesis for a better one. She —like the middle-class parent—faces forward into a future[16] that is only partially charted, and so she must furnish her children with a kind of behavior, a method of exploration, rather than with the parchment map, with its lines drawn in lovely fading colors, that is available to the teacher in the academy classroom.

The third model, the child nurse or the peasant nurse, the teacher whose task is to stay close to the young child's bodily impulses and exuberant imaginative attempts to take in the world around him, is a new type of teacher. She has come into being as one gifted thinker after another—Froebel, Montessori, Anna Freud—rebelled against the price which modern, urbanized, industrialized Europeans and Americans were paying for their new kind of civilization. From Germany, from Italy, from Vienna, from England, and from the United States there came a demand for some form of education which would fit the little child —a chair and table to fit his body, materials with which he could work out his groping attempts to relate inner and outer world,[17] and teachers who would kneel beside him, give him a shoulder to cry on or a body which could be turned into a steed, who would be allies of his infancy, rather than surrogates either of the finished world of tradition or of the fluid world-in-the-making of the entrepreneur. First in the kindergarten, and later and much more articulately in the nursery school, we have developed an educational pattern which contains some of the values of the child nurse, or the peasant nurse, in which sensitive teachers, who must almost always be young because of the strenuous physical demands of working with little children who are permitted to move about freely, are taught how to ally themselves with the immediacies of the world of the little child.

But in all three parallels which I have drawn, parallels which, like all figures of speech, impose an extra degree of order and so distort the reality—for in the teaming schoolrooms of America we find all three types of teacher and every possible blend, in every sort of situation—I have still ignored the changing children and have spoken as if the children who face these different kinds of teaching were themselves all of the same stuff as the teachers from whom they learn. If the children to be taught were of the same stuff as the teachers, we would still have a problem in initially training teachers for any one or any combination of the roles which I have outlined. The teacher who is adequately to represent the order of the past, the dignity and beauty of tradition, must, in the course of her training come to terms with her own past. The Latin lines she wrote so unwillingly, the theorems in geometry which were resented, the parents and teachers who were responsible for making her learn her lessons, must all be reëxamined, the rebellion exorcised or transformed, so that she can become the whole-hearted and resigned exponent of traditional learning.

The teacher who is to help a generation go away from and beyond their parents, who is to be forever exhorting her pupils to be up and doing, has a different task; she must relive her childhood and exchange the specificity of the demands which her parents and teacher made upon her for a new set of demands, which she will make, in the same tone of voice, upon her pupils. Where the teacher who represents the past and tradition must accept directly and finally both what she herself has been taught and those who stood for the past, the teacher who must urge her pupils to desert or surpass their parents has to abandon the matter but, in a way, keep the manner. She comes to terms during her training, if that training is to succeed, not with her own parents as they themselves were with all their weaknesses and strengths, but with the demands which parents and teachers in the abstract have a right and a duty to make on children. She must give up any overfaithful clinging to the particulars of her own past, if she is to face a roomful of children for whom it is her duty to wish a future very different from that which their own parents' lives offer them.

Congruently, the type teacher of our city and town schools today is a girl who is—in the words of the contemporary class analysis—mobile upward, moving from lower class to lower middle class, or from lower middle class to a better middle-class position. She is someone who must transcend her own past and so in a sense is the better prepared to help her pupils repudiate theirs and become mobile also. The type teacher of the academy or the academic subjects in a modern high school is, on the other hand, mobile downwards, clinging to a past she is in danger of losing, as a family that has fallen on hard days clings to the family portrait and the grandfather's clock.

The type nursery-school teacher is the girl from an upper middle-class background, who finds herself desperately out of sympathy with the verbal facility and concern with things rather than with people that seems to her a predominant characteristic of her world. Very often inarticulate and academically "slow," better able to communicate with a touch of the hand or the slant of a painted line than with words, she can become a nursery-school teacher only if she can come to sufficient terms with her own rebelliousness against adult standards—against, indeed, the whole adult world—so that while she acts as the little child's ally, she does not hold the child back. Very often the nursery-school teacher, and also the child therapist, is not a special kind of adult who has kept a closeness to his or her own childhood, which however is completely reorganized and made anew, but rather a young adult who is continuing to live out an unrealized childhood, and who, after a few years, wearies of the repetative game and becomes a supervisor, or teaches teachers, or decides it is more rewarding to deal with adults than with children. The teacher who within the school fulfills one of these roles which have a formal relationship to the child-rearing practice of the grandparent, parent, or child-nurse patterns seems to be the more successful the less she is acting out some unresolved and overdetermined past, and the more she has reassimilated and revised her past to fit into the teaching role which she has chosen.

But what then, when the teacher, of whatever type, in whatever type of school, has come to terms with her own past, has clearly seen her own role and is well equipped and ready to carry it out, year after year, as one class succeeds another in her school room—what then, when she meets, year after year, different children? In a more slowly changing society, the good teacher, the *guru* of India, for instance, is typically old, wise, patient, grown mellow with teaching the young about whom he has learned more and more each year. When the pupils remain the same, the teacher has only to keep alive her capacity for lively observation and response, and each year will add to her wisdom, her understanding, and her gentleness. But the world that the modern teacher confronts is a world in which each year serves, not to reinforce and amplify what she is slowly learning about the nature of ten-year-old boys or ten-year-old girls, or about the differences between ten-year-old boys, and ten-year-old girls —constancies which will give her something firm on which to base her methods—but serves rather to disorient her. What seemed to be true as she observed the fifth grade five years ago is no longer true; the children's behavior becomes not more predictable—as it should as she grows more experienced—but less predictable. Ten years ago older teachers expressed their bewilderment and resent-

ment at the circumstances that years of teaching were crowned not with wisdom and the gentleness that comes with wisdom, but with increasing ignorance and an accompanying shrillness of
voice and manner; they complained that children
hadn't any manners any more, were badly
brought up and undisciplined, had no respect. A
dozen other familiar complaints come readily to
mind. Today, in 1950, the phrasing is altered and
teachers now complain of the number of "disturbed children" who complicate their teaching
problems. But the terms "lack of manners," "lack
of respect," "unwillingness to work," which reflect the more moralistic tone of the past, or the
words "disturbed children," which reflect the psy-
chiatrically oriented thinking of the present, refer
substantially to the same condition. If the words
used today sound more frightening, perhaps it is
because the teachers of today are even more ap-
palled at the unpredictableness of their mysterious charges. For all these phrases are ways in
which the teacher says that each year she under-
stands her children, not more, as she might reasonably expect, but less. A kind of nightmare
reversal has been introduced into life, like an
escalator which insists on running backwards;
age and experience become not orienting factors
but disorienting ones, so that the teacher of

twenty years' experience may face her class less confidently than the teacher with only two.

This is, of course, no more than the normal accompaniment of the fantastic rate of change of the world in which we live, where children of five have already incorporated into their everyday thinking ideas that most of the elders will never fully assimilate. Within the lifetime of ten-year-olds the world has entered a new age, and already, before they enter the sixth grade, the atomic age has been followed by the age of the hydrogen bomb, differentiated from the atomic age in that many of those who failed to understand the dangers of the atom bomb are painfully beginning to take in the significance of the hydrogen bomb. Teachers who never heard a radio until they were grown up have to cope with children who have never known a world without television. Teachers who struggled in their childhood with a buttonhook find it difficult to describe a buttonhook to a child bred up among zippers, to whom fastnesses are to be breached by zipping them open, rather than fumblingly feeling for mysterious buttons. From the most all-embracing world image to the smallest detail of daily life the world has changed at a rate which makes the five-year-old generations further apart than world generations or even scores of generations were in our recent past, than people separated by several centuries were in the remote past. The children whom we bear and rear and teach are not only unknown to us and unlike any children there have been in the world before, but also their degree of unlikeness itself alters from year to year.

Faced with this unwieldy circumstance that the modern teacher becomes not more but, in a sense, less fitted to teach the longer she teaches, we then, as a society, and particularly as those of our society professionally interested in education, have a problem to solve. How can we set up some pattern which will enable the teacher to grow through the years, instead of becoming stunted and distorted, affrighted by the increasing gap between herself and her pupils, which is not a gap of chronological age but a gap of difference in period? Once recognized and named, it should be possible to devise, not refresher courses, which provide the teacher in service with new ways of looking at subject matter, but orientation excursions that would enable the teacher continually to readjust her picture of the sequences which the children she teaches have gone through and will go through. This would mean that the fifth-grade teacher would have regular opportunities to visit the prenatal and postnatal clinic, the playgrounds and parks where mothers take care of infants, so as to revise her picture of what parents are expecting of children and how they are treating them. She would also spend time in day-care centers, nursery schools, and kindergartens, learning how the kind of child with which she had once been familiar has been replaced by a child with new skills, new expectations, and new problems, all of which will take new forms when those same children reach her in the fifth grade. And as she is given a chance to change her picture of her pupils' past, so also she needs an opportunity to change her picture of their future, to visit the seventh grade, to visit high school. The fifth-grade children who face her today are forming their picture of what high school will be like from the experience of their older brothers and sisters who are in high school *now*, not on the picture of high school which their teacher carries in her head, from her own high school days or her practice teaching. And the teacher will also be given a chance, a patterned practical way, to visit other parts of her pupils' lives—Sunday school and scout meetings, and children's chaperoned movie showings; she will be encouraged to watch the television and listen to the radio programs which interest her children this year.

All of this orientation will take time; it will have to be organized and rewarded. Some of it will have to take the place of much of the present in-service credit for any sort of miscellaneous learning. It cannot simply be visiting, but must instead be supervised and interpreted by those who know what is there to be seen, who can save time by proper preparation and emphasis. But just as surely as we have needed a teacher education which permitted the prospective teacher to spend several years learning to teach, learning about her own relationship to her past and to her future, to her parents and her teachers and her peers, and to children and adolescents, so now we need a form of in-service training which will permit the teacher to keep abreast of a changing world, to be what she has every right to expect to be—a better, not a worse, teacher with the years.

This may seem radical and difficult enough, this demand for what amounts to a whole new institution of in-service training, an institution which consciously and delicately corrects for the extraordinary rate of change of the world in which we live—and yet, even this picture which I have drawn so far is, in a sense, a picture which is already almost out of date. For I have made it apply to a teacher who would in her single person reach some sort of synthesis of the three models which I have sketched, who would combine respect and love for the traditional with a willingness to open new doors and send children forth on uncharted seas, while preserving in them part of that closeness to themselves and to their imaginations characteristic of early childhood. Such a teacher, if she had the additional opportunity to keep herself eternally abreast of a changing world, with the latest song on her lips and the latest and most amazing scientific discovery to wonder about, could in a way re-create the nostalgic image of the teacher in the little red schoolhouse.

For that teacher was one to whom childish impulses were mischief, not delinquency; that teacher married and became part of the community, or lived on in a home and so, though unmarried, continued to hold babies in her arms and to know how current babies felt. That teacher presented no disturbing contrast with either the child's or the parents' world, but is dreamed of as having been part of both, in a schoolhouse sweet with the scent of new-mown hay and made lively by the frogs which the boys have smuggled in from the near-by creek. This nostalgic dream teacher, like all proper nostalgic dreams, represents an ideal which the self-conscious society can make an effort to reach, by continually making new inventions to deal with new conditions, to keep the dream at least within sight of each succeeding generation.

But meanwhile there is a further condition in the world, one that is nowhere allowed for in what I have said. In this discussion, we have assumed a system of education which communicated the whole of an accepted tradition to the growing child—in the cultures communicated by grandparents, in the type of education which we call academic. We have discussed the type of education in which a way of building a new and unknown future in a *known* way is communicated to children in parent-rearing societies, and by the teacher who typically is teaching children to forsake the content of their parents' lives and taking her methods as models, to go on and out to success. We have seen how the child nurse and the peasant nurse and the nursery-school teacher all have in common the function of keeping a child close to itself. And almost while these types were being delineated, while educators and psychiatrists and psychologists and specialists in child development and sociologists and anthropologists have been teaming up to reach a better understanding of what this educational process was in our own society now—before indeed the ink is dry or the galley of the manuscript which seemed so up to date has come back from the printer, a new urgency is upon us.

For already, before we have devised a way in which to keep our teachers abreast of life, so that they can even teach those things and in those ways which they now know how to teach, we need a new kind of teaching altogether. From the teacher of the traditional we need a reunderstanding of history[18] in the light of our new knowledge about men and their motives. We need this desperately because otherwise, under the pressure of a changed world, the past—and all that it means in models and in communication with ourselves through the use of the symbols our forebears used—may well be lost to us. From the teachers of little children we still need a cheerful willingness to preserve in the child that which is there, to tolerate an impulse long enough so that it may be regulated rather than rejected. We need not only a willingness to welcome the way in which a child unites its individual phantasy with the phantasy creatures of its culture, but we also need new inventions in which the child will be left free to integrate all through life—with the vividness and immediacy and concrete images so easily come by in childhood, so difficult to preserve into adulthood—each new experience. If we are to continue to live in this changing world, we need an art which can face it and make sense of it, not arts which are the screams of the dispossessed and the forsaken in a world they never knew. But to have such an art we need to keep alive a type of awareness which it was once enough to cherish in childhood, so that the gifted artist and philosopher might use this access later, as he built new symbols for his generation. We must devise ways not of cherishing awareness of the self a little longer, which is all that the current nursery school really tries to do and which is all that the child nurse and the peasant nurse did, but instead ways of making that early awareness a continuing part of the personality into adulthood and old age. We need, in fact, to do for many men what accidents of gift and history made possible in the occasional great geniuses of the past.[19]

And finally, and perhaps most difficult of all, we need from the teacher who has relied on teaching how a tried method can be used on new material, a totally new kind of teaching—a teaching of a readiness to use *unknown* ways to solve unknown problems.[20] We are facing a world which this adult generation is unable to grasp, to manage, to plan for. The most we may reasonably hope for is that somehow the old unsuitable methods will get us through until another generation is able to tackle the job. But throughout history, each generation has stood on the shoulders of the past, each new learning has come from an old learning, if only by way of contradiction and explicit rejection. How are we who do not know what to do, who do not know how to live in one world, who have no faintest trace of habituated capacity to operate in a world which may actually destroy itself, who do not know how to carry in our hearts the weight of those who died yesterday in Burma or who may die tomorrow in Prague, or how to cope with the spectacle of machines which can do problems which the men who design the machines could not do—how shall we, who are so unfit, prepare a generation which will begin to be fit to face the new problems which confront mankind? At first sight, it seems a hopeless dilemma, for men can teach only what they know. And yet it need not be, because what we need to teach is a technique which can perhaps be well communicated if we ourselves fully realize our own position. We need to teach our students how to think, when you don't know what method to use, about a problem which is not yet formulated. And is not that in a nutshell our actual position? So if we, who live now, can fully realize and incorporate into our every teaching word and gesture our parlous state, we will, as we transmit it to our pupils and students give them just the freedom, just the sense of an unguessed-at process which nevertheless *must be found*, which if they incorporate it, should equip them as no generation has ever been equipped to make the new inventions which are necessary for a new world.

NOTES

NOTES

1. For a more detailed discussion of the problem see Margaret Mead, *Male and Female: A Study of the Sexes in a Changing World* (New York: Morrow, 1949), Chapter I.

2. The Chinese Teacher. Minutes of the Fifth General Seminar of Research in Contemporary Cultures, November 13, 1947. Chinese Document no. 12, p. 6; no. 28, p. 13. (Unpublished.)

3. M. Zborowski, "The Place of Book-Learning in Traditional Jewish Culture," *Harvard Education Review*, XIX (Spring 1949).

4. W. L. Warner, R. Havighurst, and M. B. Loeb, *Who Shall Be Educated?* (New York: Harpers, 1944). This is an excellent statement of some of the sociological facts of the teaching profession and the teacher's role in the United States today.

5. See Chapter III, "We Are All Third Generation," in Margaret Mead, *And Keep Your Powder Dry* (New York: Morrow, 1943). David Riesman, *The Lonely Crowd* (New Haven: Yale University Press, 1950).

6. "Educative Effects of Social Environment as Disclosed by Studies of Primitive Societies," *Environment and Education: A Symposium*, Human Development Series, Vol. I, no. 54, pp. 48-61.

7. Margaret Mead, "The Implications of Culture

Change for Personality Development," *American Journal of Orthopsychiatry*, XVII (October 1947), 633-646.

8. For a discussion of the child nurse in family structure and relation to imagination see Margaret Mead, "The Family in the Future," in *Beyond Victory*, edited by Ruth Nanda Anshen (New York: Harcourt Brace, 1943). See also Margaret Mead, "Age Patterning in Personality Development," *American Journal of Orthopsychiatry*, XVII (April 1947), 231-240.

9. Margaret Mead, *Coming of Age in Samoa* (New York: Morrow, 1928). Reprinted by New American Library, 1949.

10. Gregory Bateson and Margaret Mead, *Balinese Character*. New York Academy of Sciences, Special Publications, no 11. Margaret Mead, "The Arts in Bali," *Yale Review*, XXX, 335-347.

11. Gregory Bateson, *Naven* (Cambridge: University Press, 1936) and Mead, *Male and Female*. See also Gregory Bateson, "Bali: The Value System of a Steady State," in *Social Structure: Studies Presented to A. R. Radcliffe-Brown*, edited by Meyer Fortes (Oxford: Clarendon Press, 1949).

12. Margaret Mead, "Research on Primitive Children," in *Manual of Child Psychology*, edited by Leonard Carmichael (New York: John Wiley, 1946), pp. 667-706.

13. The *babushka* and *nyanya* of prewar Russia is an excellent example of this dual role. See Geoffrey Gorer and John Rickman, *The People of Great*

Russia: A Psychological Study (London: Cresset Press, 1949).

14. Margaret Mead, *Growing Up in New Guinea* (New York: Morrow, 1930). Collected in omnibus edition *From the South Seas* (New York: Morrow, 1939). Erik H. Erikson, *Childhood and Society* (New York: Norton, 1950).

15. Mead, "Implications of Culture Change for Personality Development," *American Journal of Orthopsychiatry*, XVII, 633-646. Margaret Mead, "Character Formation and Diachronic Theory," in *Social Structure*, ed. Fortes, pp. 18-35.

16. Margaret Mead, "An Anthropologist Looks at the Teacher's Role," *Educational Method*, XXI (1942), 210-223.

17. Muriel Rukeyser, *The Life of Poetry* (New York: A. A. Wyn, 1949). Miss Rukeyser has suggested the word "*in*vironment" as a literal translation of Claud Bernard's *milieu interieur* for this inner world in contrast to the environment. See also Edith Cobb, *The Therapeutic Function of the Creative Fantasy in Childhood during Latency Period: A Study of the Psycho-biological Basis of Semantics* (New York: Survey Social Work, 1947).

18. Caroline F. Ware, editor, *The Cultural Approach to History* (New York: Columbia University Press, 1940).

19. Margaret Mead, "Some Relationships between Social Anthropology and Psychiatry," to be published in *Dynamic Psychiatry* by Chicago University Press; Margaret Lowenfeld, "The Nature

and Use of the Lowenfeld World Test in Work with Children and Adults," *Journal of Psychology*, XXX (October 1950), 325-331; Ernst Kris, "The Function of Drawing and the Meaning of the Creative Spell in the Schizophrenic Artist," *Psychoanalytic Quarterly*, XV (1947), 6-31.

20. Gregory Bateson, "Experiments in Thinking about Observed Ethnological Material," *Philosophy of Science*, VIII (January 1941), 53-68. George F. Lombard, "Self-Awareness and Scientific Method," *Science*, CXII (September 15, 1950), 289-293. T. H. Huxley and Julian Huxley, *Touchstone for Ethics* (New York: Harpers, 1947).